30 days DRAWING ANIMALS
LIKE AN ARTIST

OF_____

Patricia Rogers

Patricia Rogers, a prominent figure in the realm of anime artistry, is renowned for her exceptional talent in crafting engaging anime and manga illustrations targeted specifically at children. Born and raised in the vibrant landscapes of America, Patricia discovered her passion for art at a young age, finding inspiration in the colorful world of anime.

At the age of 38, Patricia has established herself as a distinguished artist and author, captivating young audiences with her unique approach to teaching the art of drawing anime and manga. Her creative journey has led her to author several instructive books tailored for children, aiming to nurture budding artists and ignite their passion for the captivating realm of anime.

With a keen eye for detail and a profound understanding of the nuances of anime aesthetics, Patricia's artwork resonates with readers, bringing to life vibrant characters and enchanting narratives. Her dedication to the art form is evident in the intricate brushstrokes and vivid colors that grace the pages of her creations.

In addition to her artistic pursuits, Patricia is a fervent advocate for art education in schools, believing in the transformative power of creativity in shaping young minds. Through workshops, school visits, and online tutorials, she shares her knowledge and expertise, inspiring countless aspiring artists to explore the boundless possibilities of anime art.

Despite her achievements, Patricia remains humble and deeply passionate about her craft. Her commitment to empowering the next generation of artists continues to drive her artistic endeavors, making her a beloved figure in the world of anime and manga.

Patricia Rogers stands as a testament to the limitless potential of creativity and remains a guiding light for young artists, inspiring them to dream big and explore the endless horizons of anime art.

EMBARKING ON THE ARTISTIC ADVENTURE: PERFECT FOR BUDDING ARTISTS!

THIS BOOK IS TAILORED FOR THOSE WHO ARE JUST SETTING OUT ON THEIR DRAWING JOURNEY. ITS UNIQUE TEACHING METHOD BLENDS **80%** CLEAR INSTRUCTIONS WITH **20%** ROOM FOR YOUR IMAGINATION TO SOAR. IT'S LIKE A MAGICAL TREASURE MAP WHERE YOU GET TO EXPLORE AND DISCOVER YOUR ARTISTIC PATH!

BUT THAT'S NOT ALL – CONSIDER THIS BOOK YOUR PERSONAL COMPASS IN THE VAST WORLD OF ART. WONDERING WHAT YOU TRULY ENJOY DRAWING? MANY BEGINNERS FACE THIS CHALLENGE. FEAR NOT, FOR I AM HERE TO GUIDE YOU, MY DEAR FRIEND! LET'S UNRAVEL THE MYSTERIES OF ART TOGETHER AND FIND YOUR PASSION. YOUR ARTISTIC ADVENTURE STARTS HERE!

DRAWING IS LIKE CREATING MAGIC ON PAPER USING JUST A PENCIL. IT'S THE ART OF MAKING PICTURES BY DRAWING LINES AND SHAPES, AND IT'S ALL ABOUT LETTING YOUR IMAGINATION RUN WILD! IMAGINE TURNING A SIMPLE SHEET OF PAPER INTO A WORLD FULL OF ENDLESS POSSIBILITIES.

WITH DRAWING, YOU CAN EXPRESS YOUR FEELINGS, THOUGHTS, AND DREAMS WITHOUT USING WORDS. IT'S LIKE TELLING A STORY THROUGH PICTURES, WHERE YOU ARE THE AUTHOR, ILLUSTRATOR, AND HERO ALL AT ONCE! THERE ARE SO MANY EXCITING WAYS TO DRAW, AND EACH ONE IS LIKE A SECRET DOOR TO A NEW ADVENTURE.

1. **PENCIL AND INK MAGIC:** IMAGINE USING YOUR PENCIL LIKE A WIZARD'S WAND, CREATING AMAZING WORLDS AND CHARACTERS WITH JUST A STROKE OF YOUR HAND.

2. **CHALK AND CHARCOAL MYSTERIES:** DIVE INTO THE SHADOWS AND LEARN THE ART OF BLENDING AND SHADING, GIVING YOUR DRAWINGS DEPTH AND LIFE.

3. **COLORFUL CRAYON QUESTS:** TRAVEL THROUGH A RAINBOW OF COLORS, BRINGING YOUR DRAWINGS TO LIFE WITH VIBRANT HUES AND BRILLIANT SHADES.

4. **DIGITAL ART ADVENTURES:** EXPLORE THE WORLD OF DIGITAL ART, WHERE YOU CAN CREATE STUNNING ARTWORKS ON YOUR COMPUTER, MAKING MAGIC WITH TECHNOLOGY.

5. **CARTOON CAPERS:** ENTER THE WORLD OF CARTOONS, WHERE CHARACTERS COME TO LIFE WITH EXAGGERATED FEATURES AND PLAYFUL PERSONALITIES.

REMEMBER, THERE ARE NO RULES IN ART—JUST ENDLESS OPPORTUNITIES TO EXPLORE, EXPERIMENT, AND CREATE SOMETHING TRULY MAGICAL. SO GRAB YOUR PENCIL, GATHER YOUR COLORS, AND LET YOUR IMAGINATION SOAR. THE WORLD OF DRAWING IS WAITING FOR YOUR UNIQUE TOUCH!

HAVE YOU EVER WONDERED WHY PEOPLE LOVE TO DRAW?

It's not just about putting pencil to paper; it's like opening a door to a world of endless possibilities and excitement!

1. RELAX AND UNWIND: Drawing isn't just about making pictures; it's a way to relax your mind and let your imagination run free. It's like taking a little vacation for your brain!

2. CAPTURE THE WORLD: Imagine turning ordinary things you see every day into magical designs and colors. Drawing helps us see the beauty in the world and bring it to life on paper.

3. PRESERVE MEMORIES: Have you ever wanted to keep a special moment forever? Drawing lets you turn your memories into beautiful artworks, like a personal time capsule of happiness.

4. EXPRESS YOURSELF: Sometimes, words can't capture how we feel inside. Drawing helps us express our emotions, turning them into colorful masterpieces that speak volumes without saying a word.

5. BOOST YOUR BRAIN: Drawing isn't just fun; it's like a workout for your brain! It improves your hand-eye coordination, making your hands and eyes work together like a superhero team.

6. SOLVE PUZZLES WITH ART: Did you know that drawing can make you a better problem solver? It sharpens your mind, making you great at finding creative solutions to challenges.

7. FEEL CONFIDENT: As you draw and see your skills grow, you'll feel more confident in your abilities. It's like leveling up in a video game but in the real world!

8. MAKE MASTERPIECES: Did you know famous artists like Leonardo da Vinci and Vincent van Gogh started as young artists like you? With practice, you can create your own masterpieces too!

SO, GRAB YOUR PENCILS AND LET YOUR CREATIVITY SOAR! DRAWING ISN'T JUST A HOBBY; IT'S A SUPERPOWER THAT MAKES THE WORLD A MORE COLORFUL AND EXCITING PLACE!

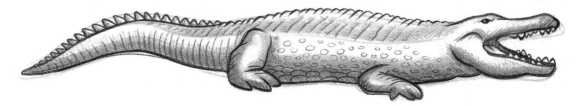

HEY THERE, BUDDING ARTISTS!

Embarking on this artistic journey is like stepping into a magical realm where your imagination knows no bounds! As you dive into the world of drawing, remember: **THE FIRST 30 DAYS** are your foundation, your canvas waiting to be filled with endless possibilities.

1. EMBRACE THE LEARNING: Every stroke of your pencil is a step toward mastery. Don't worry about perfection; instead, relish the process of learning and growing. With each drawing, you're honing your skills and discovering your unique style.

2. CONSISTENCY IS KEY: Just like a superhero hones their powers through practice, your drawing skills get stronger with every sketch. Dedicate time each day to draw—whether it's a few minutes or an hour, your commitment will fuel your progress.

3. EMBRACE MISTAKES: Don't fear mistakes; they are the stepping stones to improvement. Each smudged line and erased mark is a lesson, guiding you toward perfection. Embrace them, learn from them, and watch how they transform into your greatest strengths.

4. FIND INSPIRATION: Seek inspiration everywhere! Nature, books, movies, or even your dreams—inspiration can strike from the most unexpected places. Let your surroundings fuel your creativity and infuse life into your artwork.

5. CELEBRATE PROGRESS: Acknowledge your achievements, no matter how small they may seem. Every drawing is a victory, a testament to your dedication. Celebrate your progress, and let it inspire you to reach even greater heights.

6. STAY CURIOUS: Curiosity is your best friend on this artistic adventure. Explore different styles, experiment with various techniques, and never stop asking questions. The more you explore, the richer your artistic vocabulary becomes.

7. PATIENCE AND PERSEVERANCE: Rome wasn't built in a day, and neither is a masterpiece. Be patient with yourself. Your artistic journey is a marathon, not a sprint. Stay persistent, and you'll be amazed at how far you've come.

REMEMBER, YOUR CREATIVITY HAS NO LIMITS. WITH EVERY STROKE OF YOUR PENCIL, YOU'RE CRAFTING A WORLD THAT IS UNIQUELY YOURS. SO, EMBRACE THE CHALLENGE, STAY CURIOUS, AND LET YOUR CREATIVITY SOAR. YOUR ARTISTIC ODYSSEY BEGINS NOW—ENJOY EVERY MOMENT OF IT!

WHAT YOU NEED

Imagine you want to be a rock star, strumming your guitar like a pro. But guess what? The fanciest guitar won't make you a musical genius overnight, right? Well, the same rule applies to art! Some young artists worry about having the most high-tech art supplies, thinking it'll instantly make them professional artists. But here's the secret: it's not about the tools you use; it's all about how you use them and how creative you can get.

Just like finding your perfect guitar style takes practice and experimenting with different guitars, discovering your art style comes from trying out various pencils, brands, and techniques. So, don't be afraid to explore! Your creativity is the real magic ingredient when you're drawing! Let your imagination run wild and have fun experimenting with different tools and ideas. Who knows? You might discover your unique artistic style along the way!

PAPER

It's heart-wrenching to see someone pour their heart and soul into a drawing, only to find it on a flimsy piece of notebook paper. Here's a golden tip: invest in a Bristol Smooth drawing paper pad! It's like upgrading from a bike to a sleek motorcycle. This paper is thick and robust, perfect for all your artistic adventures. It can handle all the erasing and redrawing you throw at it without breaking a sweat. Imagine it as the perfect canvas that makes your drawings shine brighter and smoother. So, why settle for a bumpy road when you can cruise on a smooth highway of creativity?

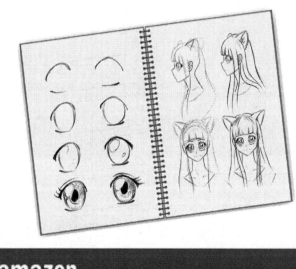

PENCIL, PENS, RULERS!

Choosing your art tools is like picking your favorite ice cream flavor - it's all about what feels right for you! Pencils come in different types - some are harder, and some are softer. But watch out, the softer ones can smudge more easily. The first things to consider are how hard the pencil is and its quality. Personally, I like using a regular No. 2 pencil, but you should try a bunch to find what feels perfect in your hand. Your pencil should be your buddy, fitting just right and not getting dull or messy over time.

Now, let's talk about pens! Art stores have a bunch of cool pens you can choose from. Each pen tip creates a different line, so don't limit yourself to super thin lines. Instead, get a variety of pens with different tip widths - it's like having a whole team of superheroes with different powers! And hey, for those long lines, a 15-inch ruler is your superhero tool. Make sure it's transparent plastic so you can see your drawing while you work. Now, armed with your perfect pencils, pens, and ruler, you're ready to create your artistic masterpieces!

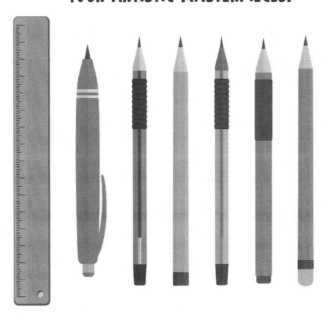

PENCIL SHARPENERS, ERASERS

Let's talk about some cool tools to make your drawings awesome! First up, pencil sharpeners. You know what? The simple handheld sharpeners you find at school or in your art kit work better than those fancy electric ones. They keep your pencils sharp and are super easy to use - just like sharpening a sword before a big adventure!

Now, onto kneaded erasers! These are like magic erasers for artists. Need to erase a big area? Kneaded erasers are your superheroes! You can find them at art stores. They're big, soft, and leave way less pink dust on your paper. Sure, they might not always be super precise, but here's a trick: use a smaller pencil eraser along with them, and you'll have the perfect team to erase anything you want in your drawings!

amazon prime

kneaded erasers for artists

Deliver to Robert - Port Reading 07064

Here's the key: never give up! The real magic happens when you practice drawing a lot! It's like planting seeds in a magical garden. The more you draw, the more your skills grow, just like flowers blooming in spring. So, keep going, be patient, and believe in yourself. Before you know it, you'll see your art skills reaching for the stars!

CROSSHATCHING

Picture this: using a special technique called crosshatching can transform your drawing into a masterpiece! It's like adding a sprinkle of magic to your artwork. The key trick? Pay attention to the spaces between your lines - that's what makes it really awesome! Just like connecting the dots in a puzzle, these lines come together to create something truly amazing. So, grab your pencils and let the crosshatching adventure begin! Your drawings will shine brighter than ever!

CROSSHATCHING DRAWING

MASTERING THE ART OF CROSS-HATCHING MIGHT SOUND TRICKY, BUT IT'S NOT AS HARD AS IT SEEMS. THERE ARE A FEW KEY THINGS YOU NEED TO KNOW TO GET IT RIGHT:

HAVE CONFIDENCE IN YOURSELF! DON'T FEAR MAKING MISTAKES - IT'S OKAY TO BE WRONG SOMETIMES!

CONSISTENT PRACTICE IS THE KEY! MAKE IT A HABIT TO DRAW FOR AT LEAST AN HOUR EVERY DAY, AND WITHIN A MONTH, YOU'LL SEE INCREDIBLE PROGRESS!

UNLOCK YOUR FULL POTENTIAL! INVEST YOUR TIME IN MASTERING COMPLEX OBJECTS BY FIRST PERFECTING SIMPLE ONES. THE FOUNDATION OF INTRICATE DRAWINGS LIES IN MASTERING THE BASICS!

SMOOTH HAND MOVEMENTS ARE KEY! YOU DON'T NEED TO PRESS TOO HARD WITH THE PENCIL. GENTLE STROKES ON THE PAPER WILL GIVE YOU THE PERFECT OUTCOME

CROSSHATCHING VARIETIES

- BASIC CROSSHATCHING
- ADDITIONAL CROSSHATCHING
- COMPLEX TYPES OF CROSSHATCHING

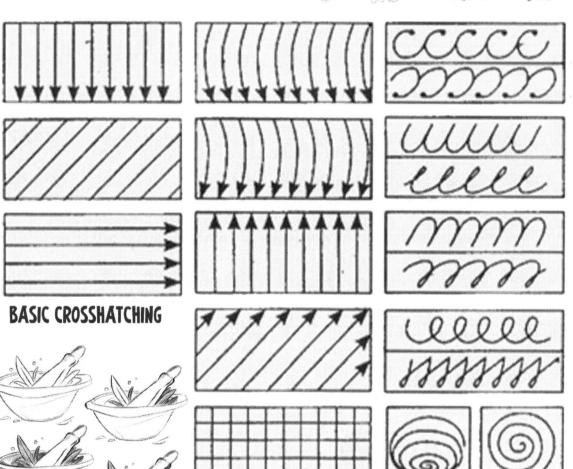

BASIC CROSSHATCHING

ADDITIONAL CROSSHATCHING

COMPLEX TYPES OF CROSSHATCHING

SKETCH HATCHING

Get ready for a cool journey into the world of shading with pencils! I'm going to show you some awesome shading styles and the right way to make those hatches. It's like adding magic shadows to your drawings - are you excited to learn the secrets?

TRAIN YOUR SKILLS

1, Take a deep breath and chill out!
2, Let your hand loosen up, like it's dancing!
3, Ready to follow my awesome art guide?

Activity 1: Start by drawing with the lightest touch, as if your pencil is floating on air. Then, give it another go and see your drawing come to life!

TRAIN YOUR SKILLS

Hey there, super artists! Don't stress if things don't go perfectly on your first try! Mistakes are just detours on the creative adventure!

Tip: Repeat this activity for a few days! It's a good idea to have a special workbook where you can practice these exercises. Think of it as your magical art journal!

TRAIN YOUR DRAWING SKILLS

SKETCH HATCHING MAGIC: YOU MIGHT THINK THIS ACTIVITY SOUNDS DULL AT FIRST, BUT WAIT UNTIL I SPRINKLE SOME EXCITEMENT INTO IT! MANY FOLKS OVERLOOK ITS IMPORTANCE, BUT TOGETHER, WE'LL TURN THIS EXERCISE INTO A SUPER FUN AND UNIQUE ADVENTURE!

IMAGINE A MAGICAL SKETCHBOOK WHERE YOU CAN BRING YOUR CREATIVE IDEAS TO LIFE!

TRAIN YOUR DRAWING SKILLS

TRAIN YOUR DRAWING SKILLS

TRAIN YOUR DRAWING SKILLS

TRAIN YOUR DRAWING SKILLS

TRAIN YOUR DRAWING SKILLS

TRAIN HAND MOTOR SKILLS

EXPLORE THE WORLD OF ROUND SHAPES!

Diving into the world of round shapes can be a super fun adventure for budding artists like you! Why, you ask? Well, practicing patterns with round shapes isn't just a creative exercise; it's like a magical key that unlocks your artistic abilities.

The coolest part? As you keep drawing those round shapes, your hand becomes friends with the pencil, making you the master of your art tools. It's like training for a big art adventure! And guess what? These round patterns aren't just dots on a page; they add a sprinkle of magic to your artwork. They create depth, making your drawings pop with excitement and energy.

TRAIN HAND MOTOR SKILLS

So, let your imagination soar as you explore the endless world of round shapes! With every circle, you're not just drawing; you're building a masterpiece, one curve at a time. Let the fun and creativity flow!

TRAIN HAND MOTOR SKILLS

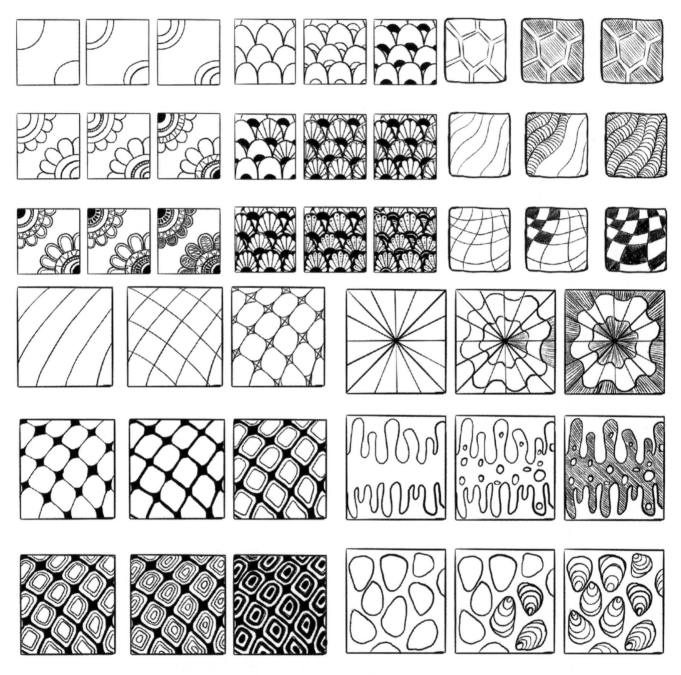

IMAGINE THIS: EVERY TIME YOU DRAW A ROUND SHAPE, YOU'RE NOT JUST MAKING A CIRCLE; YOU'RE BUILDING YOUR UNDERSTANDING OF SHAPES AND FORMS. IT'S LIKE CONNECTING THE DOTS OF CREATIVITY! PLUS, PLAYING AROUND WITH THESE ORGANIC, FLOWING LINES ISN'T JUST ABOUT DRAWING; IT'S ABOUT DANCING YOUR PENCIL ON THE PAPER, CREATING PATTERNS THAT COME TO LIFE.

TRAIN HAND MOTOR SKILLS

BASICS OF SHADING

Observe how the levels on the value scale correspond to the shading in the drawing.

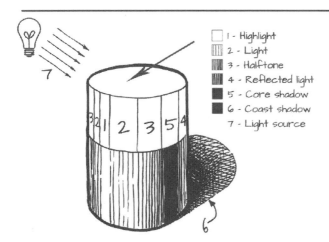

1 - Highlight
2 - Light
3 - Halftone
4 - Reflected light
5 - Core shadow
6 - Coast shadow
7 - Light source

Identify your **LIGHT SOURCE**. Where the light hits your object will be the **HIGHLIGHT** or the lightest **VALUE**.

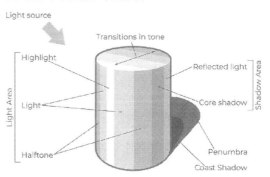

Light source

Transitions in tone

Highlight

Light Area

Light

Halftone

Reflected light

Core shadow

Shadow Area

Penumbra

Coast Shadow

5 WAYS TO SHADE:
1. Stipple 2. Hatch 3. Cros Shatch 4. Scribble 5. Blend

1.STIPPLE
USE SMALL DOTS TO CREATE **VALUE**.

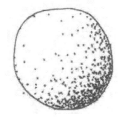

2.HATCH
USE PARALLEL LINES TO CREATE **VALUE**.

3.CROSS HATCH
USE CROSSING LINES TO CREATE**VALUE**.

4.SCRIBBLE
USE LOOPED, CROSSED, SCRIBBLE LINES TO CREATE **VALUE**.

5.BLEND
COLOR IN THE SHADOW, THEN SMOOTH IT OUT TO CREATE **VALUE**.

VALUE SCALE:
SHOWS THE RANGE FROM THE DARKEST VALUES TO THE LIGHTEST VALUES IN EVEN STEPS.

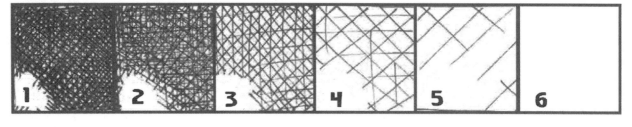

TRAIN SHADING SKILLS

Experiment with five different shading techniques provided below. Utilize the arrows as a reference for the direction of the light source, guiding you on where to place highlights and shadows.

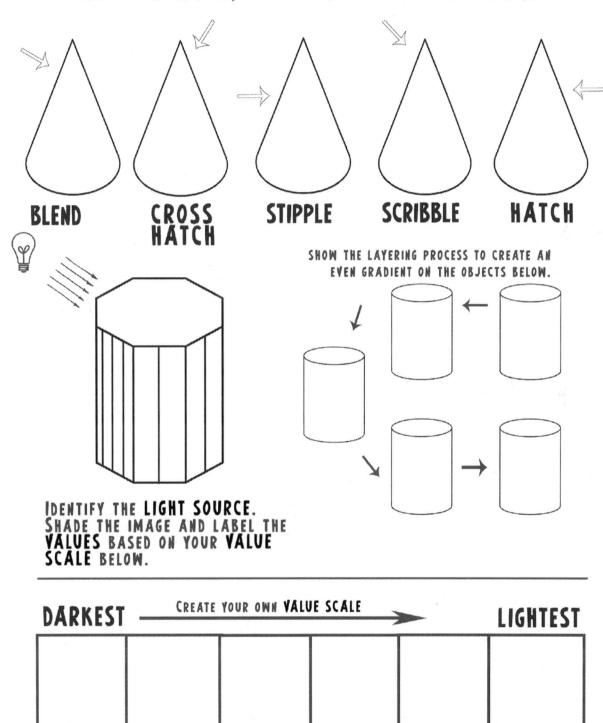

BLEND **CROSS HATCH** **STIPPLE** **SCRIBBLE** **HATCH**

Show the layering process to create an even gradient on the objects below.

Identify the **LIGHT SOURCE**. Shade the image and label the **VALUES** based on your **VALUE SCALE** below.

DARKEST → Create your own **VALUE SCALE** → **LIGHTEST**

1	2	3	4	5	6

TRAIN SHADING SKILLS

REPEAT AS ABOVE!

1. STIPPLE
USE SMALL DOTS
TO CREATE **VALUE**.

TRAIN SHADING SKILLS

2.HATCH
Use parallel lines to
create **Value**.

3.CROSS
HATCH
Use crossing lines to
create **Value**. **Value**.

TRAIN SHADING SKILLS

4. SCRIBBLE
USE LOOPED, CROSSED, SCRIBBLE LINES TO CREATE **VALUE**.

5. BLEND
COLOR IN THE SHADOW, THEN SMOOTH IT OUT TO CREATE **VALUE**.

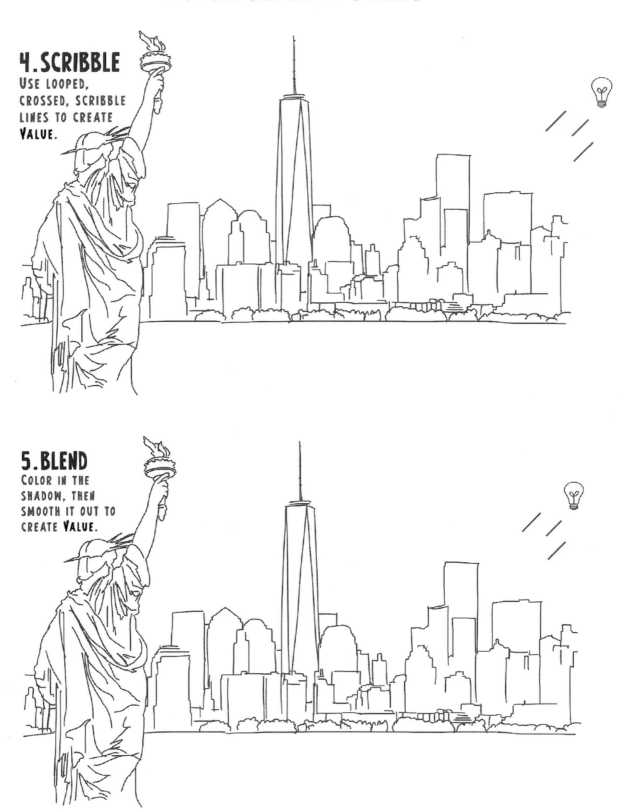

TRAIN SHADING SKILLS

TRAIN SHADING SKILLS

Levek UP!

LET'S TALK ABOUT GEOMETRIC SHAPES!

Geometric shapes might sound simple, but they are the building blocks of art and design. Imagine circles, squares, triangles, rectangles, and ovals – these are the superheroes of art! When you learn to play with these basic shapes, you unlock a world of creative possibilities.

For budding artists like you, mastering these shapes is like getting the keys to an artist's toolbox. They help you understand cool techniques like perspective, shading, and how to arrange things on your canvas. You see, drawing these shapes isn't just about lines and curves; it's about grasping the secrets of form, space, and

But here's the exciting part: these shapes are not just your ordinary tools. They're like magic seeds that, when combined and rearranged, can grow into fantastic, complex drawings! Picture this: you can transform a simple circle into a smiling sun or a square into a sturdy castle.

When you explore these shapes, you're not just improving your drawing skills; you're also nurturing your creativity. By mixing and matching, you can invent amazing designs you never thought possible! So, dive into the world of geometric shapes, young artists, and let your creativity soar! Who knows what extraordinary masterpieces you'll create?

DRAW CUBE

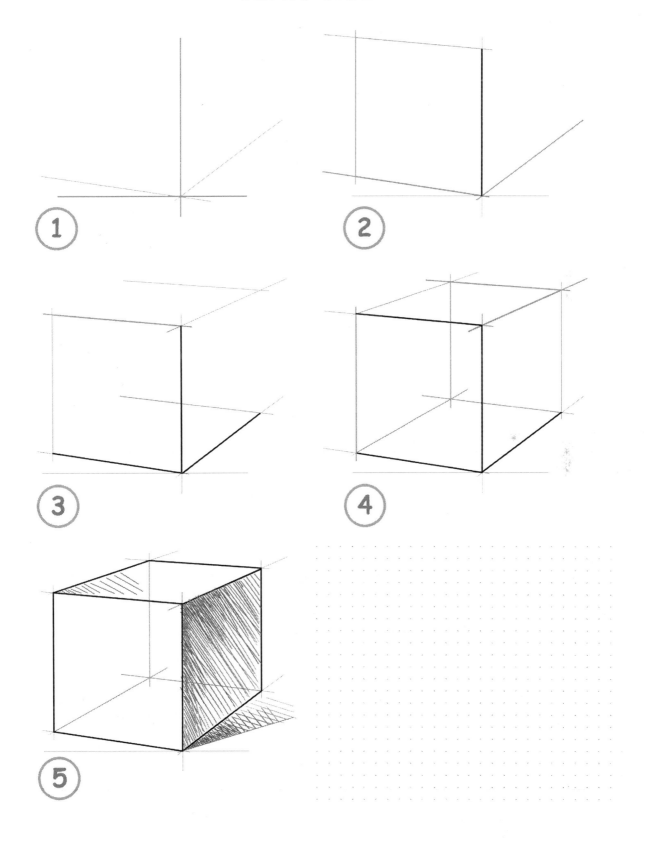

DRAW A BALL

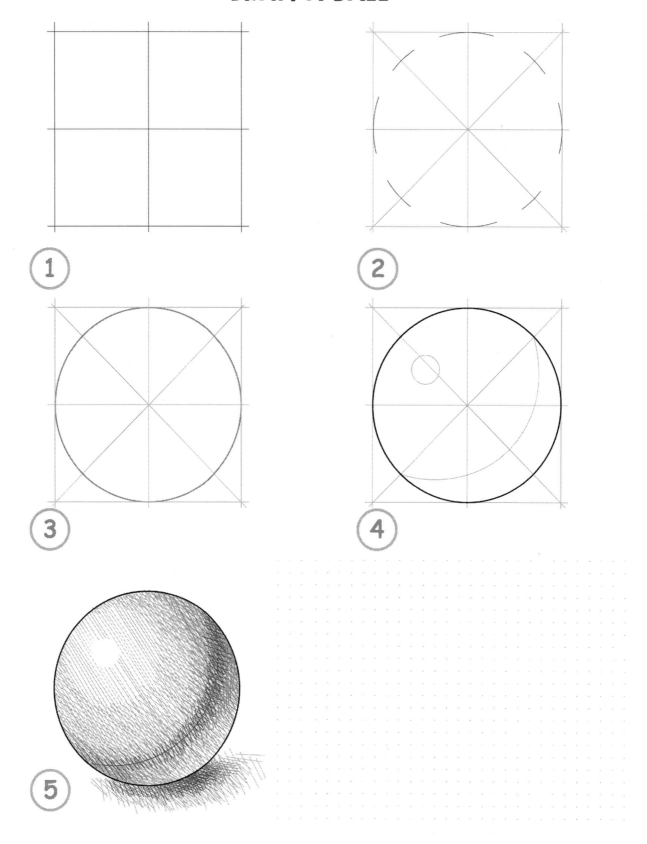

DRAW A CYLINDER

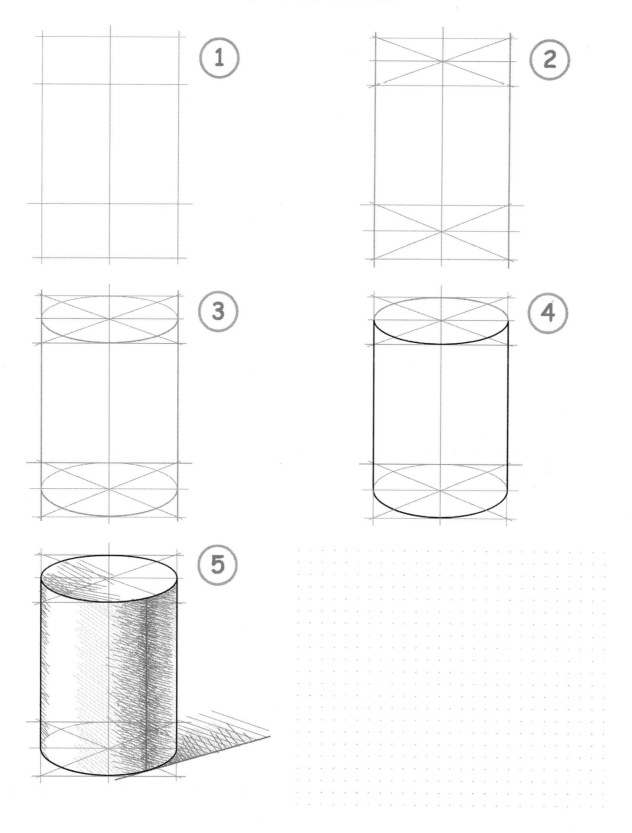

DRAW A CYLINDER AND CUBE.

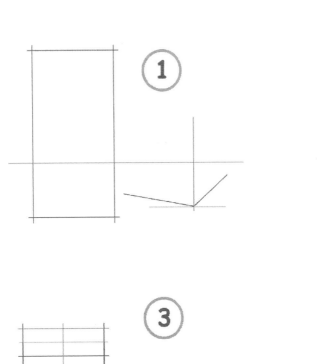

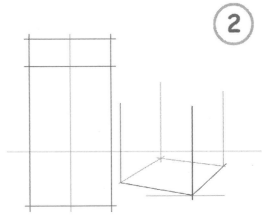

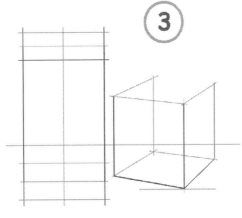

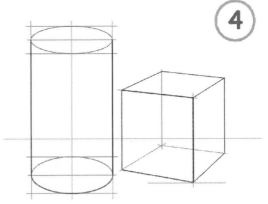

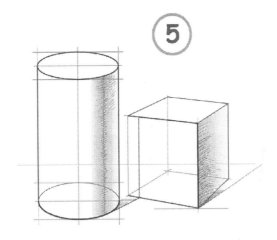

DRAW A STEP-WISE SKETCH

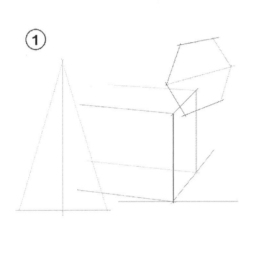

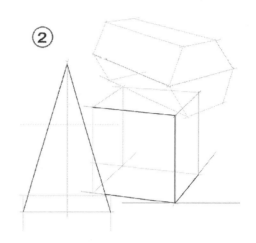

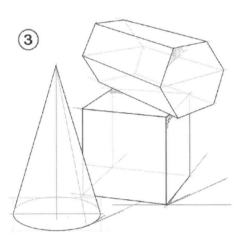

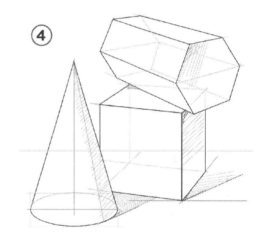

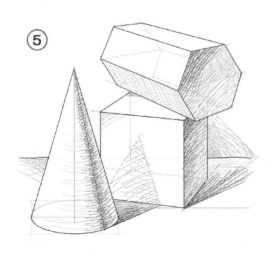

DRAW A BAL AND CUBE.

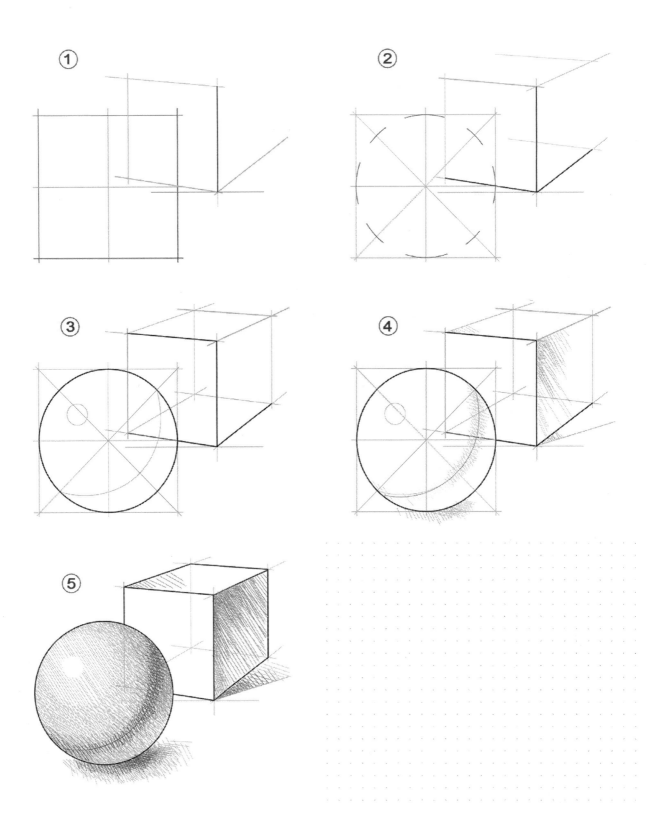

DRAW A PYRAMIDS

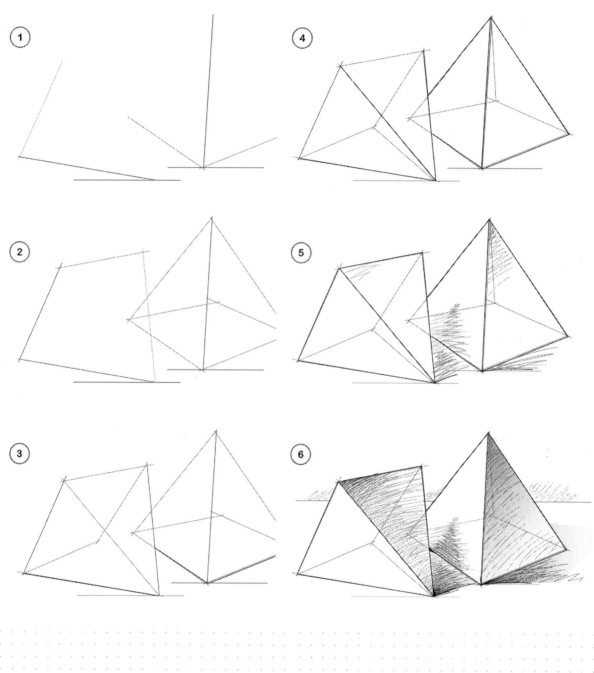

EXPLORE THE WORLD THROUGH YOUR DRAWINGS!

DID YOU KNOW THAT LEARNING TO DRAW A WIDE RANGE OF THINGS IS LIKE LEARNING A MAGICAL LANGUAGE? IMAGINE BEING ABLE TO DRAW NOT JUST ONE OR TWO THINGS, BUT EVERYTHING AROUND YOU! IT'S LIKE HAVING A SUPERPOWER THAT HELPS YOU SEE THE WORLD IN A WHOLE NEW WAY.

FOR BUDDING ARTISTS, DRAWING DIFFERENT OBJECTS IS LIKE EMBARKING ON EXCITING ADVENTURES. IT'S NOT JUST ABOUT LINES AND SHAPES; IT'S ABOUT UNLOCKING THE MYSTERIES OF FORM, TEXTURE, AND BALANCE. WHEN YOU DRAW DIVERSE OBJECTS, YOU'RE NOT JUST CREATING ART; YOU'RE BUILDING YOUR OWN VISUAL DICTIONARY. YOU CAN DRAW ANYTHING - FROM A PLAYFUL PUPPY TO A TOWERING TREE - AND MAKE IT COME TO LIFE ON PAPER.

BUT HERE'S THE REAL MAGIC: DRAWING EVERYTHING HELPS YOU DISCOVER YOUR UNIQUE STYLE. IT'S LIKE FINDING YOUR OWN ARTISTIC FINGERPRINT! BY EXPERIMENTING WITH DIFFERENT SUBJECTS, YOU FIND WHAT RESONATES WITH YOU, CREATING A STYLE THAT'S AS SPECIAL AND UNIQUE AS YOU ARE.

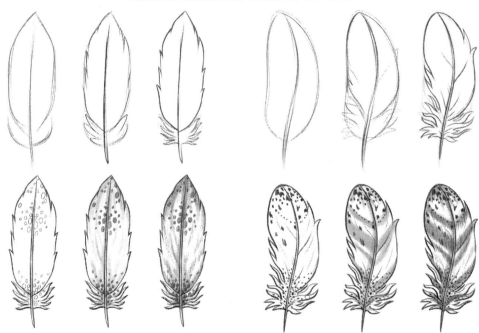

DRAWING ISN'T JUST ABOUT MAKING PICTURES; IT'S ABOUT EXPLORING YOUR PASSIONS AND INTERESTS. THROUGH YOUR ART, YOU CAN EXPRESS WHAT MAKES YOU EXCITED AND CURIOUS ABOUT THE WORLD. IT'S LIKE GOING ON A TREASURE HUNT, UNCOVERING NEW SKILLS AND TALENTS ALONG THE WAY.

SO, YOUNG ARTISTS, GRAB YOUR PENCILS AND LET'S EMBARK ON THIS ARTISTIC JOURNEY! DRAW EVERYTHING YOU SEE AND DREAM ABOUT. WITH EACH STROKE, YOU'RE NOT JUST DRAWING OBJECTS; YOU'RE OPENING DOORS TO ENDLESS CREATIVE POSSIBILITIES. HAPPY DRAWING!

IMPORTANT!

GET READY FOR AN EXCITING ARTISTIC CHALLENGE! STARTING NOW, WE WILL BE DIVING INTO FULL-PAGE DRAWINGS WITHOUT ANY PRACTICE SPACES. WHY, YOU ASK? BECAUSE THIS WAY, YOU CAN SEE ALL THE INTRICATE DETAILS OF YOUR ARTWORK MORE CLEARLY!

SO, GRAB YOUR SKETCHBOOK AND LET'S GET STARTED! DON'T FORGET TO WRITE DOWN THE DATE ABOVE EACH DRAWING. IT'S LIKE MARKING THE MILESTONES OF YOUR ARTISTIC JOURNEY.

✨AND GUESS WHAT? AFTER 30 DAYS OF DRAWING, YOU'LL WITNESS HOW MUCH COOLER YOUR DRAWINGS HAVE BECOME! 🎨

ARE YOU READY TO EMBARK ON THIS AMAZING ADVENTURE? LET'S CREATE SOME ART MAGIC!

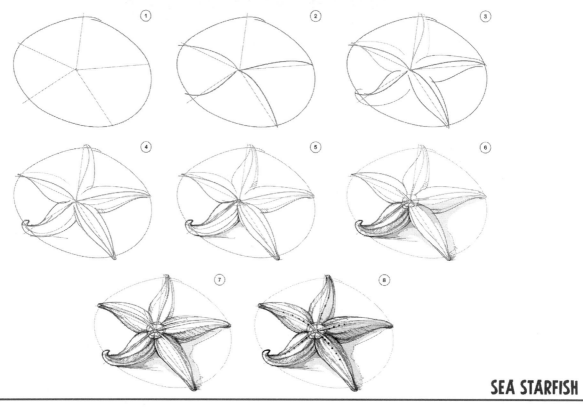

SEA STARFISH

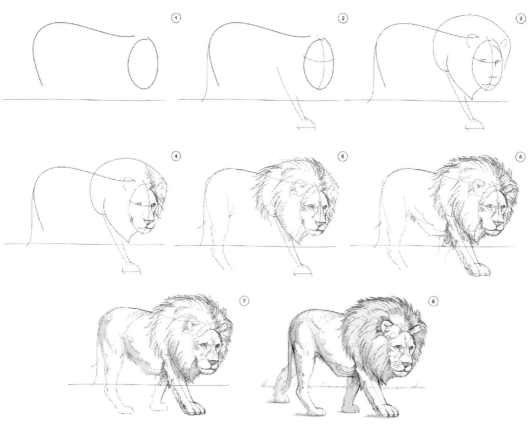

LION

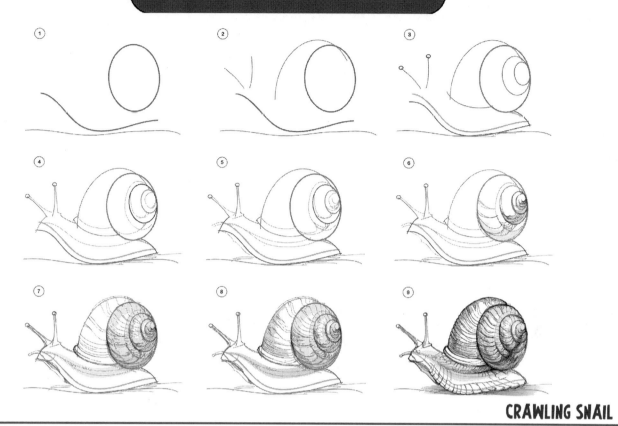

CRAWLING SNAIL

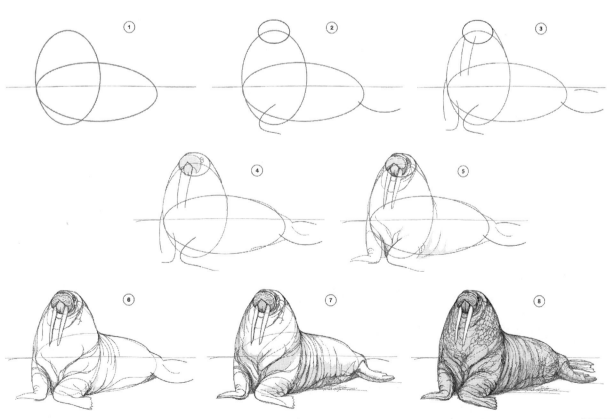

WALRUS

49

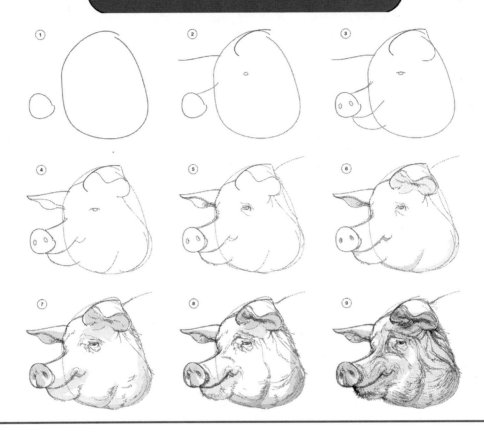

HEAD OF PIG

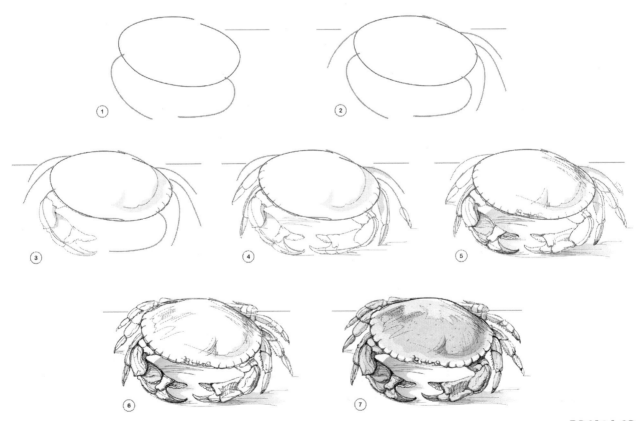

BROWN CRAB

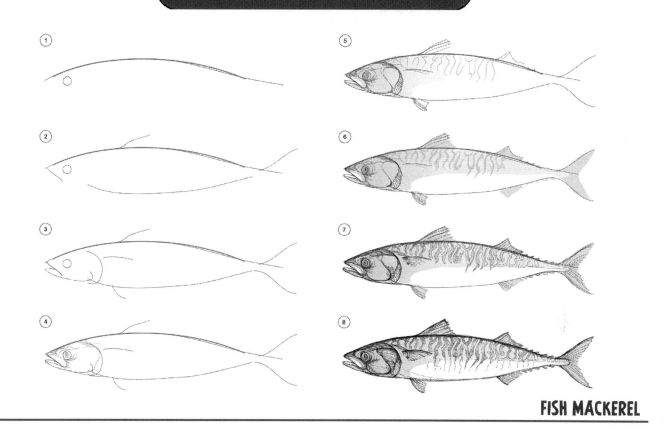

FISH MACKEREL

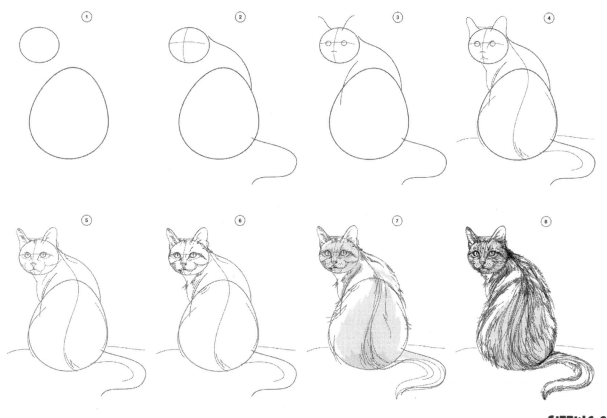

SITTING CAT

51

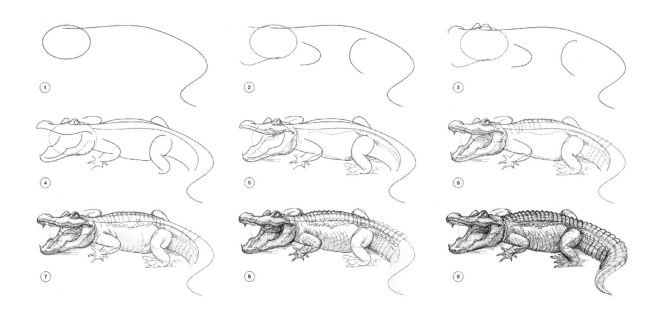

REDOUBTABLE ALLIGATOR

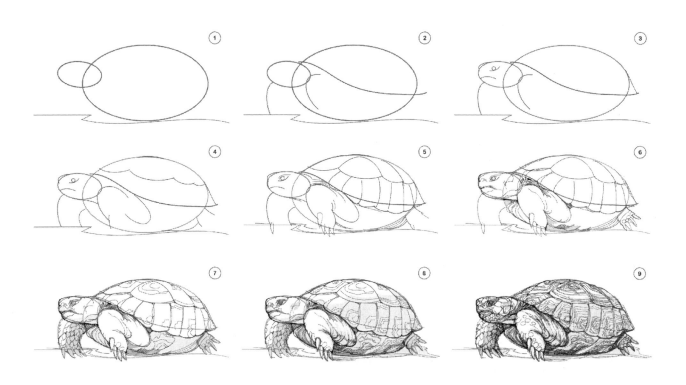

TURTLE

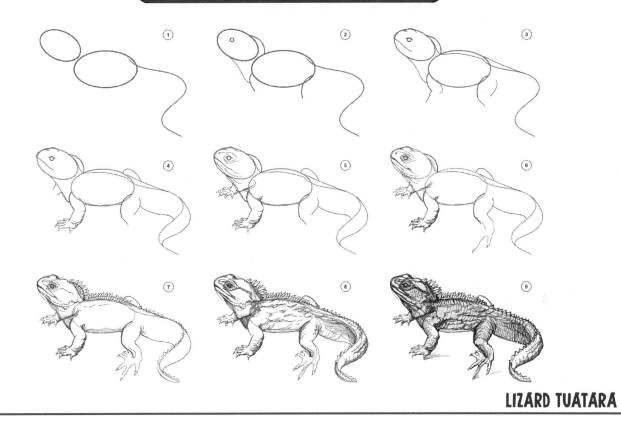

LIZARD TUATARA

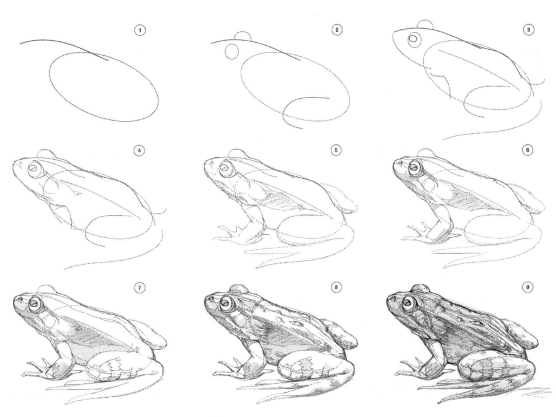

REALISTIC FROG

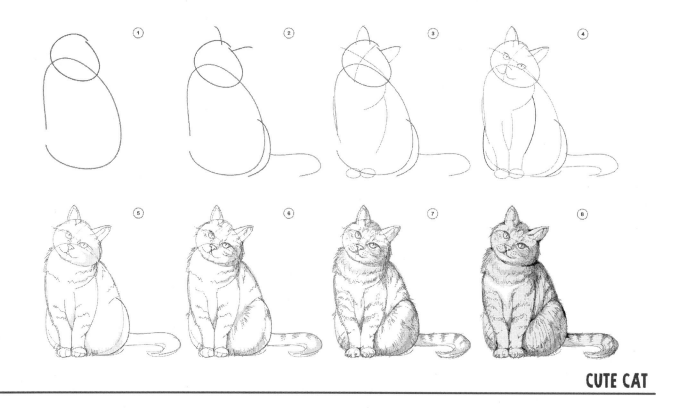

CUTE CAT

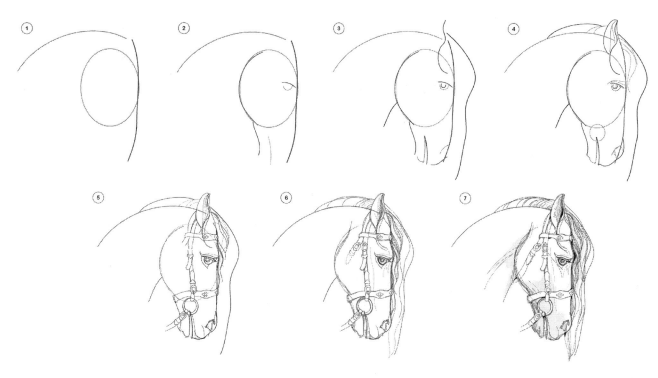

HORSE HEAD

RHINOCEROS

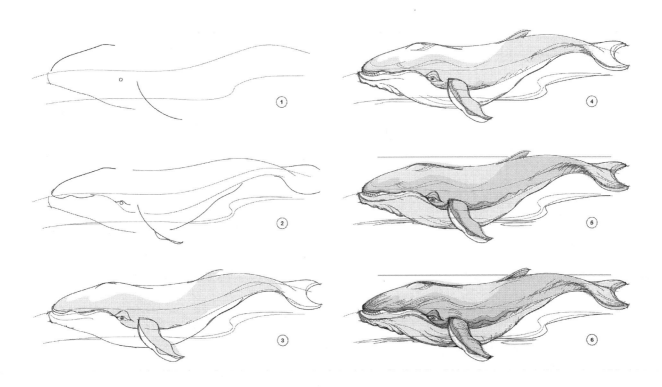

WHALE

CUTE TIGER

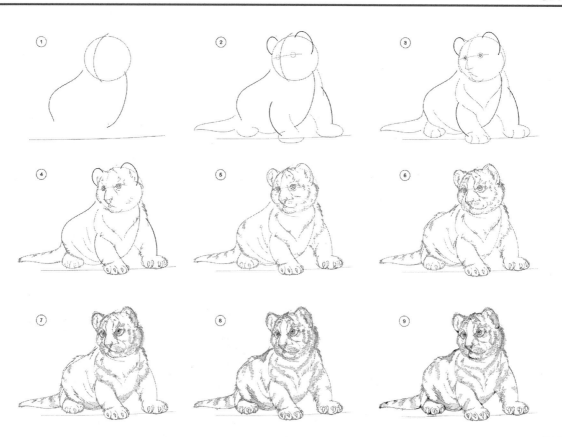

TIGER CUB

CUTE PENGUIN

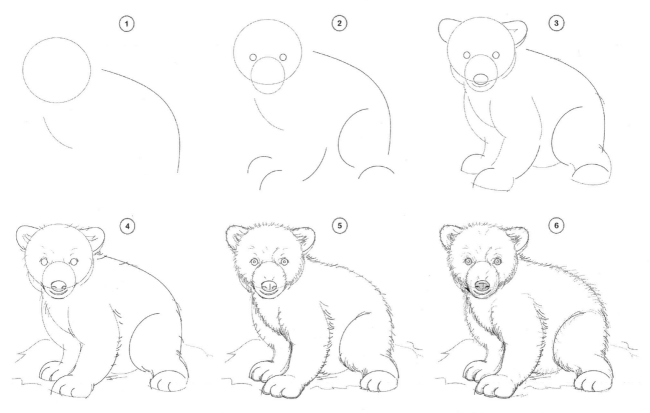

TEDDY BEAR

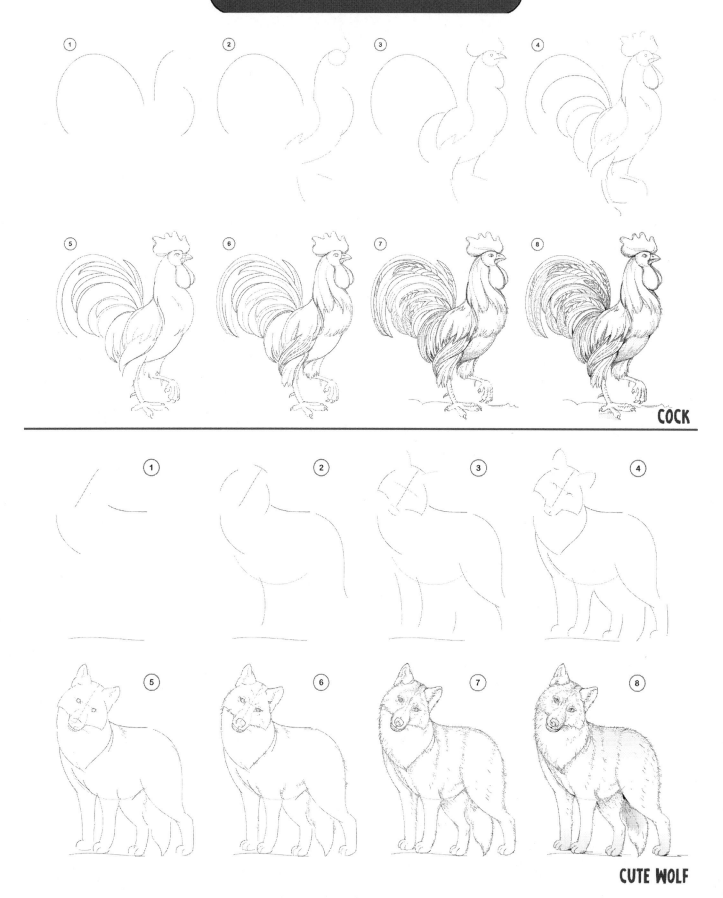

COCK

CUTE WOLF

SPARROWS

GOOSE ON FARM

59

IMAGINARY INSECT

BUTTERFLY

WHITE SHARK

HORSES

DRAW ANIMALS

CUTE RAT

AFRICAN ELEPHANT

LITTLE RABBIT

DOMESTIC PIG

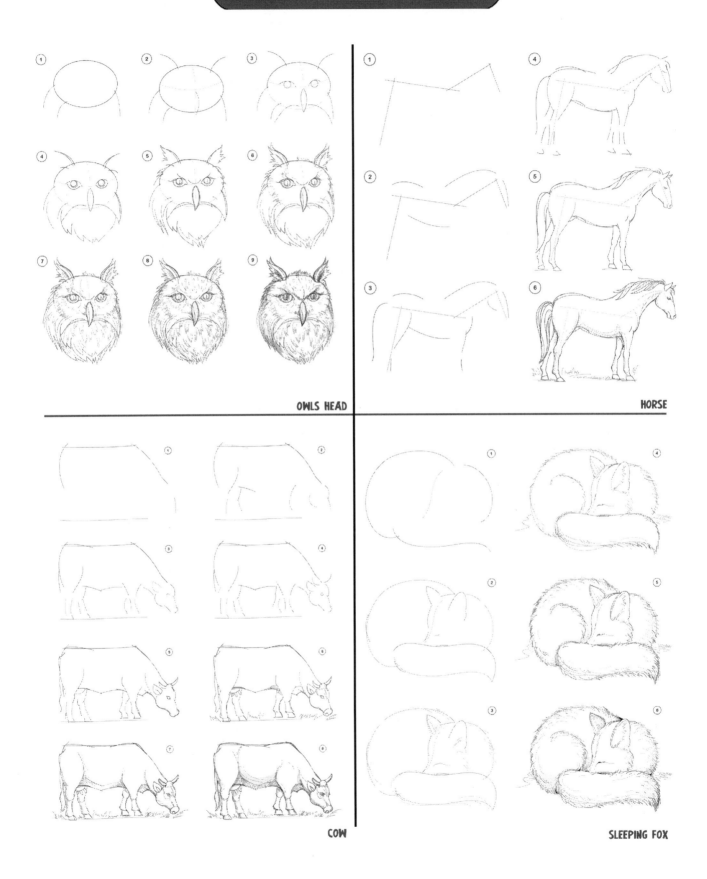

OWLS HEAD

HORSE

COW

SLEEPING FOX

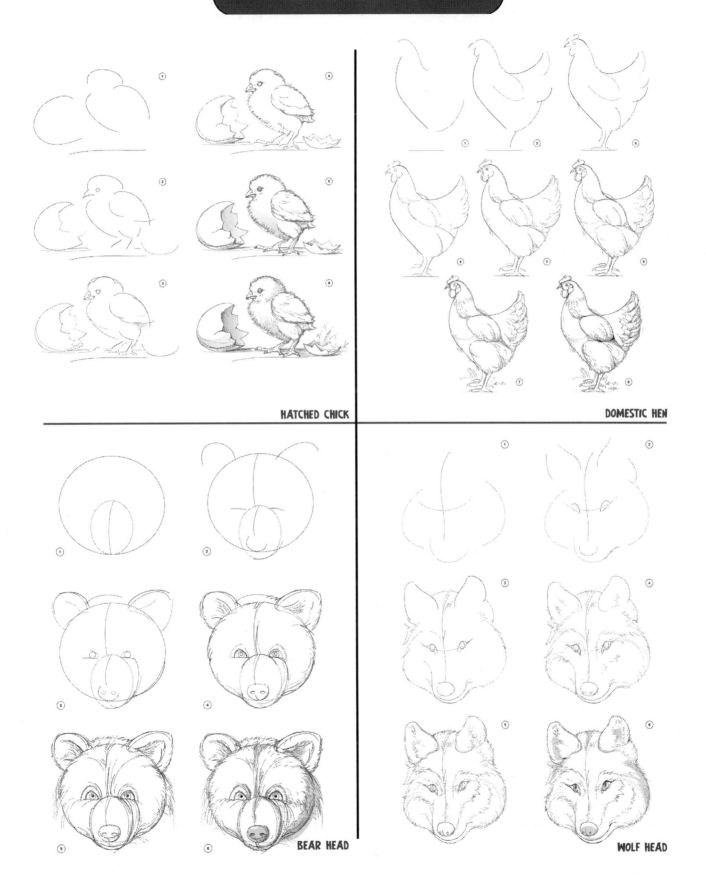

HATCHED CHICK

DOMESTIC HEN

BEAR HEAD

WOLF HEAD

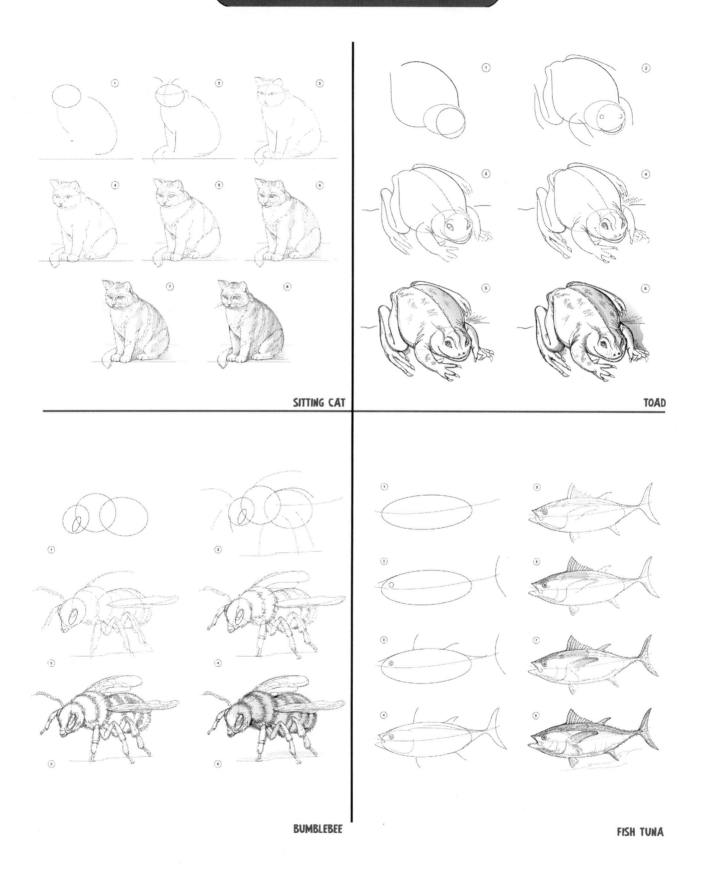

SITTING CAT

TOAD

BUMBLEBEE

FISH TUNA

IMPORTANT!

Now, a new chapter on drawing different animals begins. **DON'T BE SURPRISED THAT THE DRAWING STYLE VARIES-IT'S INTENTIONAL.** This approach makes learning more productive. Your brain gets accustomed to different drawing styles, enhancing the learning process. That's why each chapter presents drawings in various styles.

Welcome to the exciting world of animals! In this chapter, you'll embark on a thrilling adventure to learn how to draw a variety of animals. From playful puppies to majestic lions, you'll explore the diverse animal kingdom. And guess what? Each animal comes to life in its unique style, making your drawing journey even more fascinating!

Remember, diversity in drawing styles is like adding different colors to your palette. It enriches your artistic skills and opens your mind to endless creative possibilities. So, grab your pencils, and let's dive into the captivating world of animal art! Get ready to unleash your creativity and draw animals like never before!

DOE

OWL

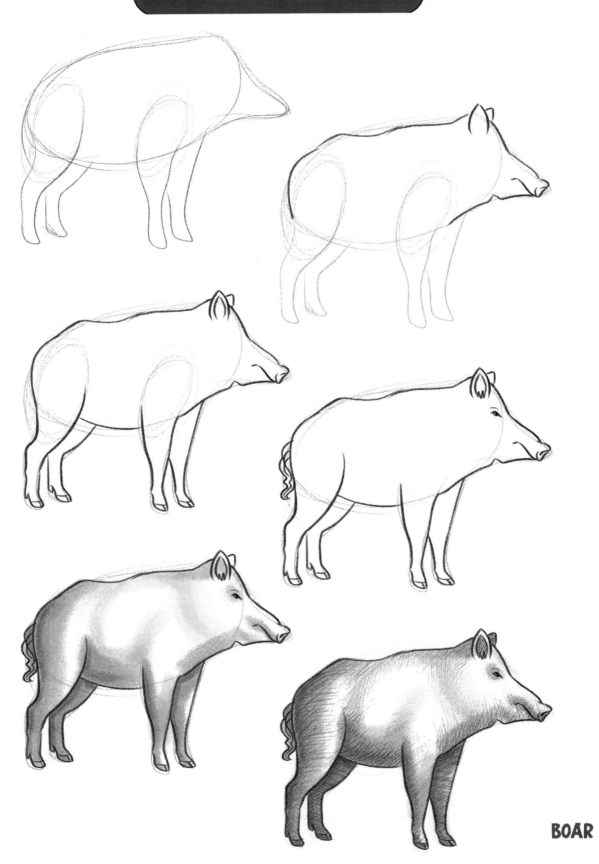

BOAR

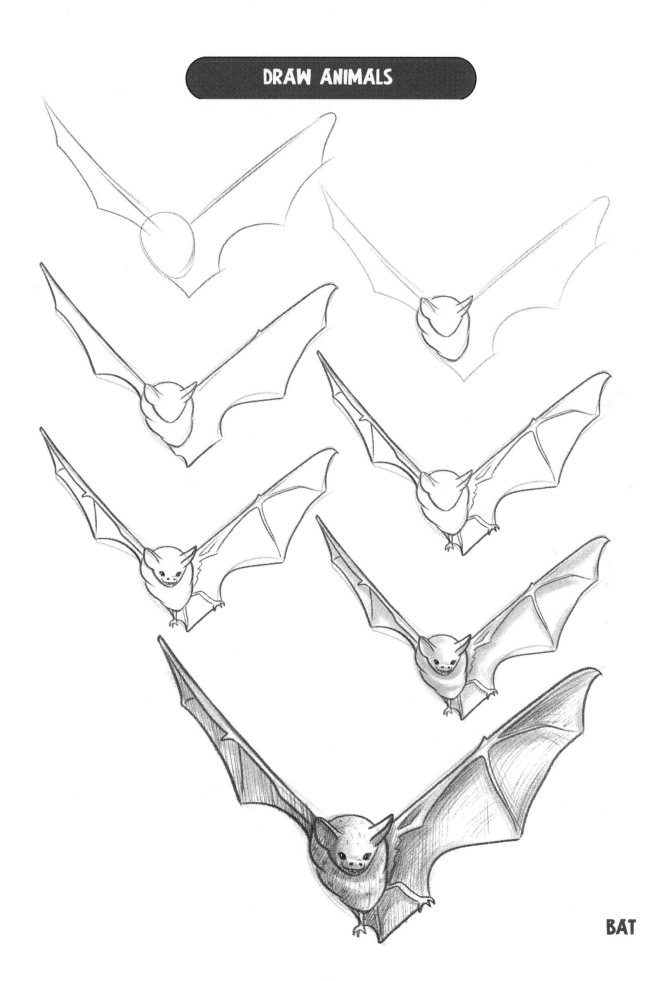

BAT

TIGER CUB

TIGER CUB

TIGER

TIGER

A LION

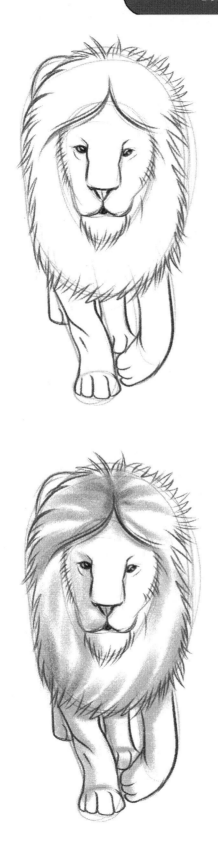

A LION

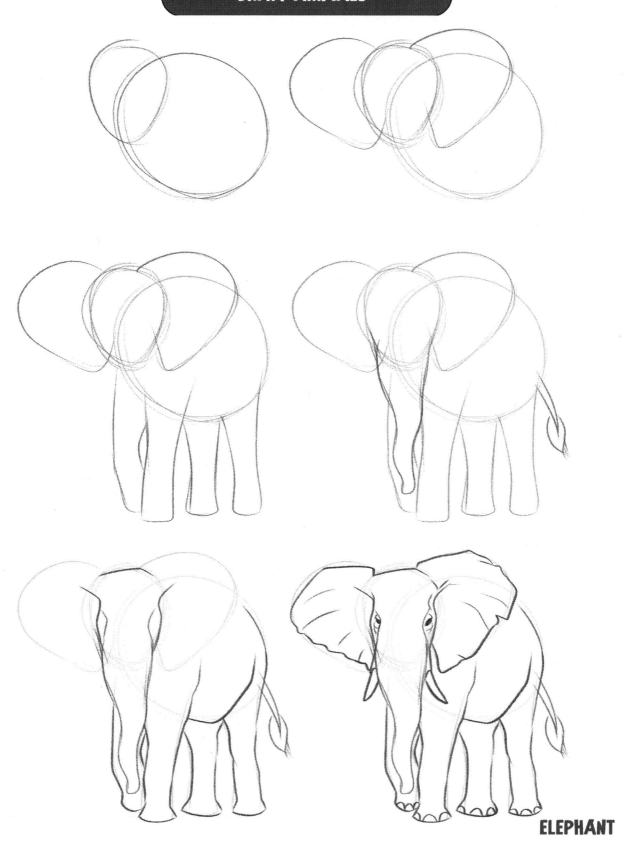

ELEPHANT

ELEPHANT

LION HEAD

DEER

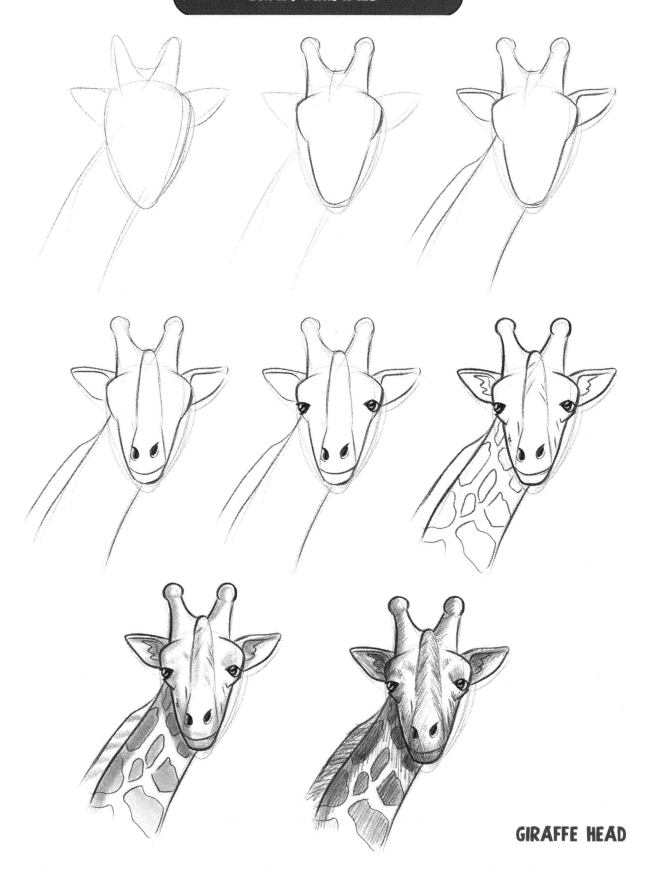

GIRAFFE HEAD

GRIZZLY HEAD

FOX HEAD

BULL'S HEAD

ELEPHANT HEAD

ZEBRA HEAD

GIRAFFE

OSTRICH

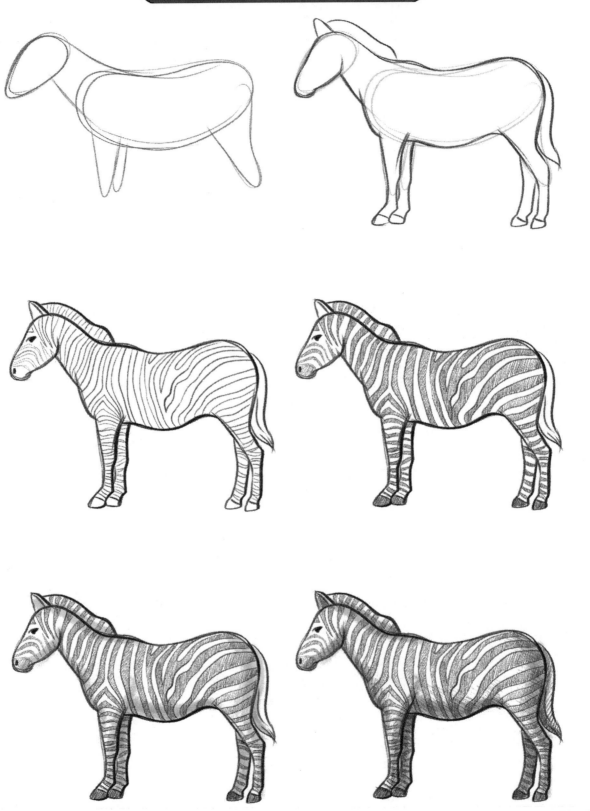

ZEBRA

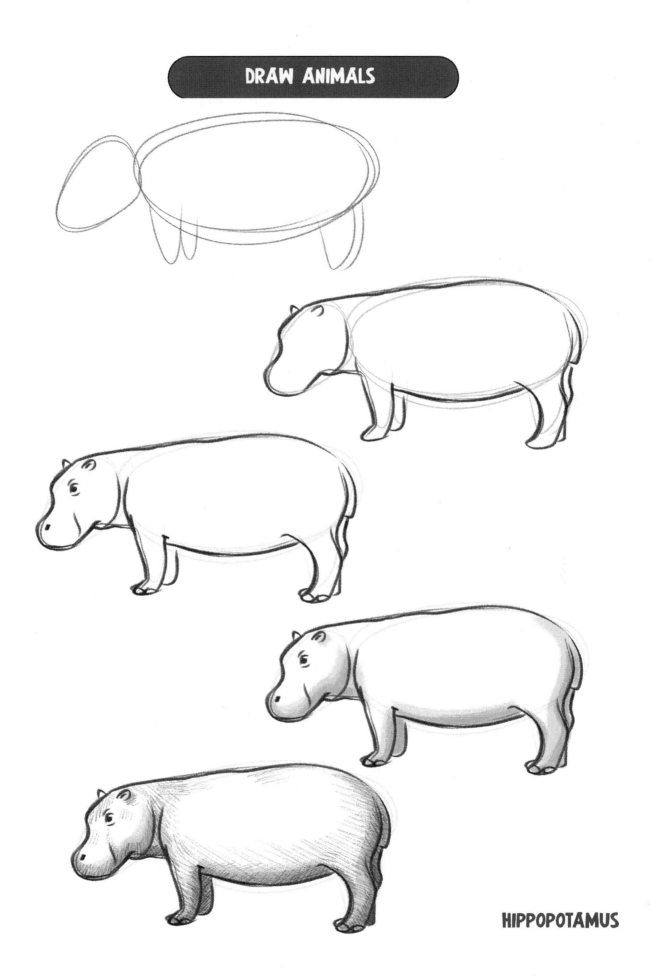

HIPPOPOTAMUS

A LION

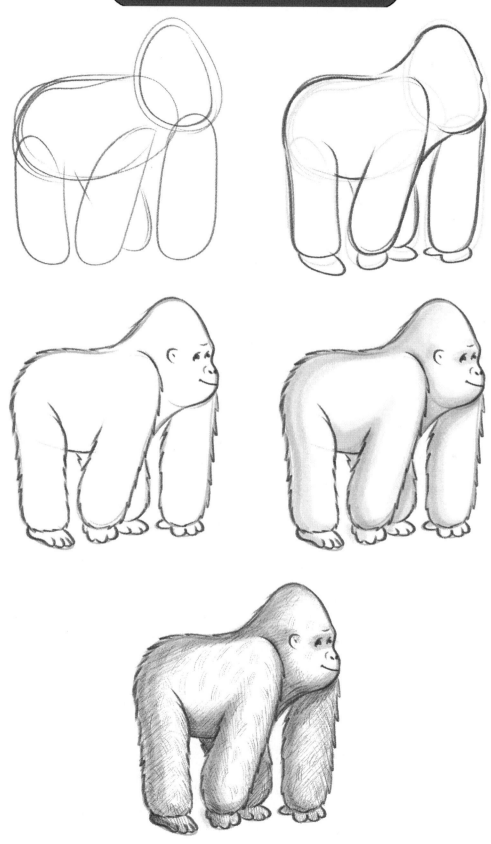

GORILLA

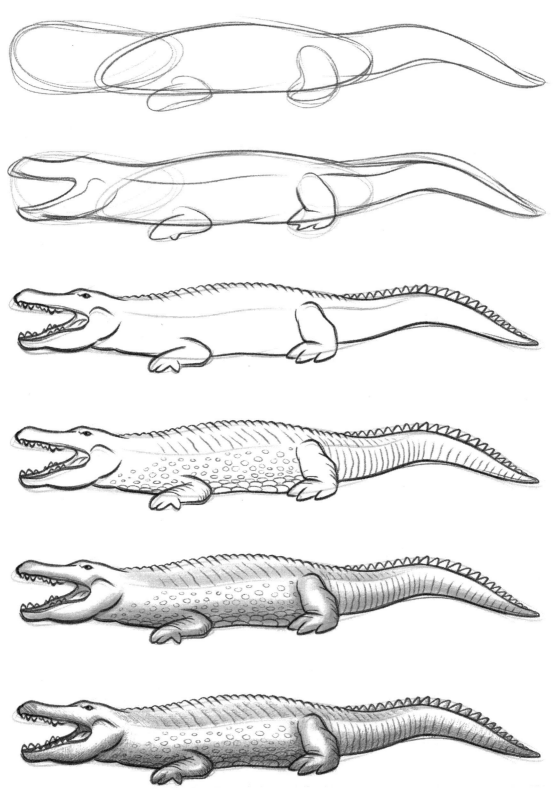

CROCODILE

CHEETAH

ELEPHANT

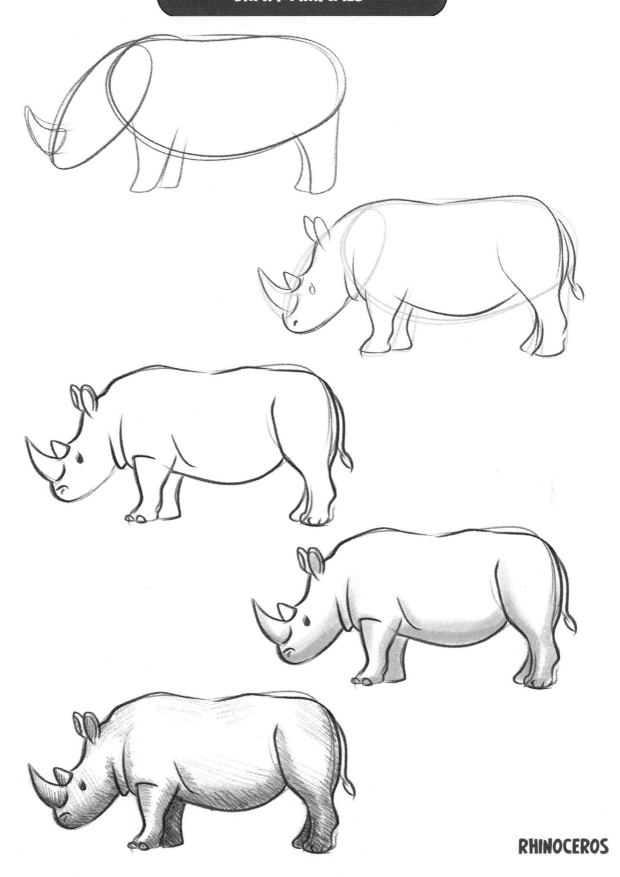

RHINOCEROS

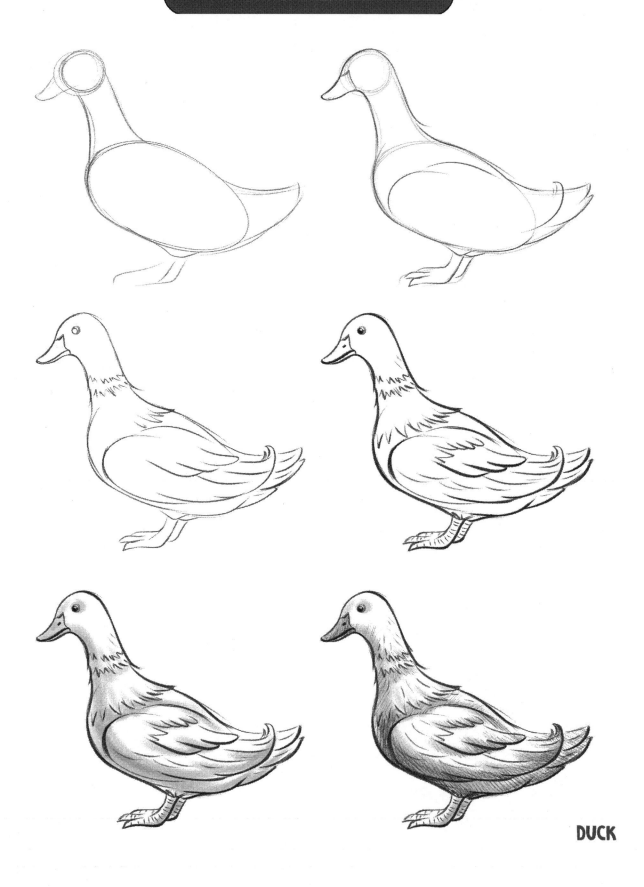

DUCK

CROW

BIRD FEATHER

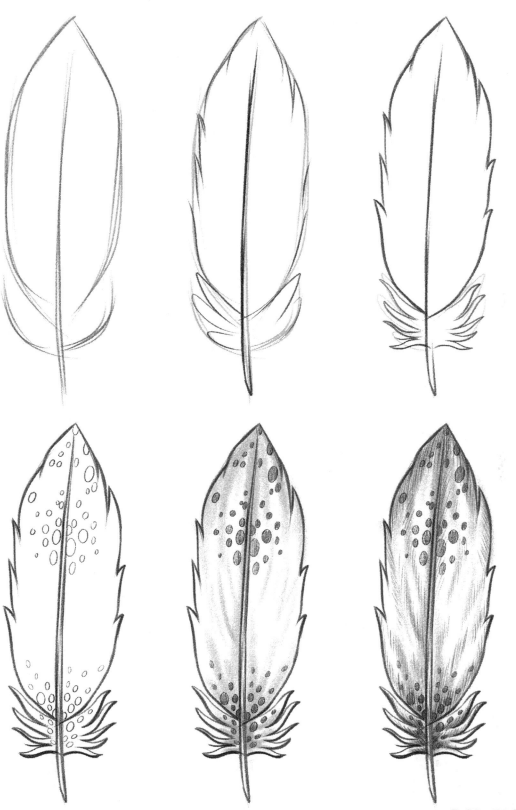

BIRD FEATHER

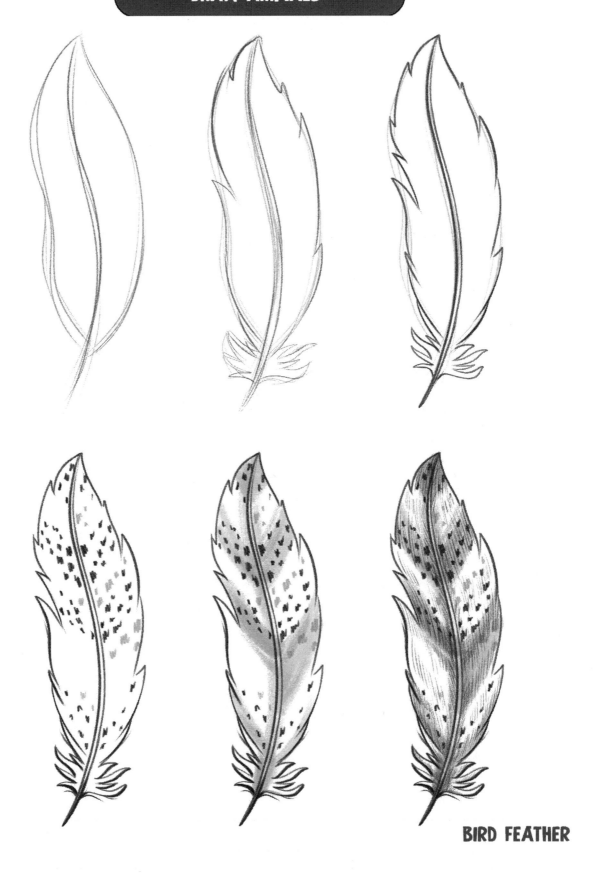

BIRD FEATHER

BIRD FEATHER

REALISTIC BUTTERFLY

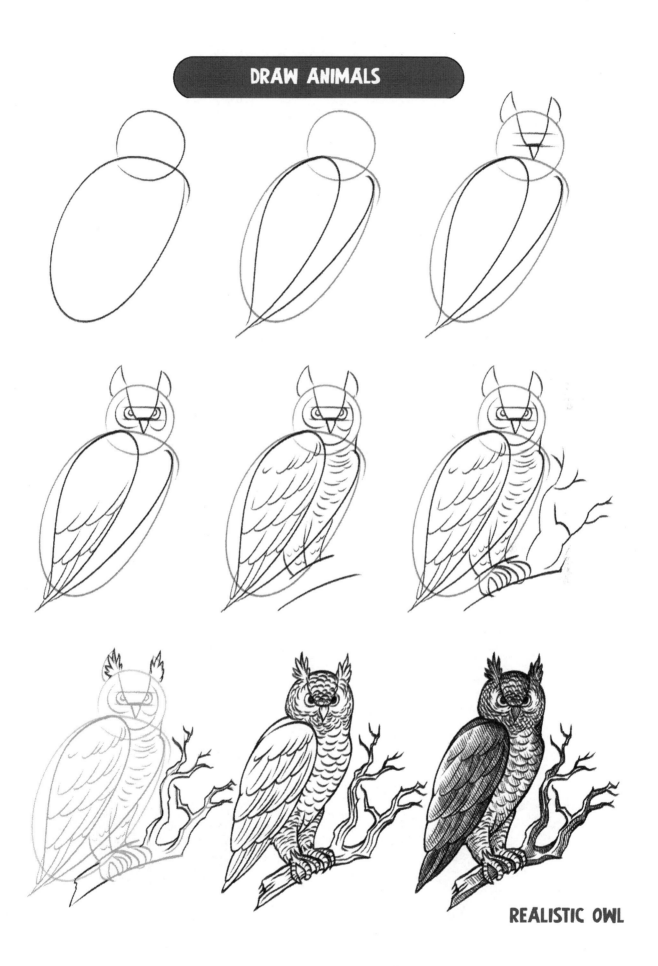

REALISTIC OWL

REALISTIC MOTH

REALISTIC RAVEN

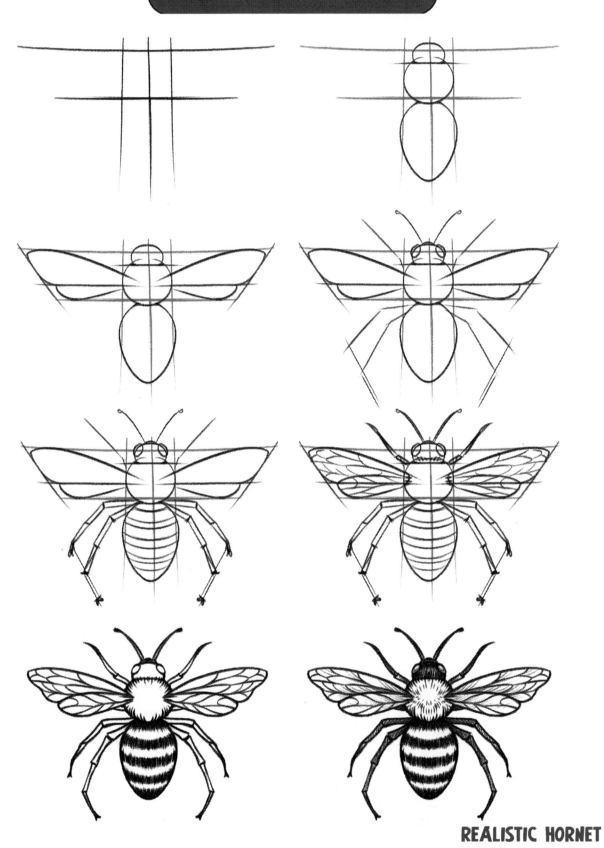

REALISTIC HORNET

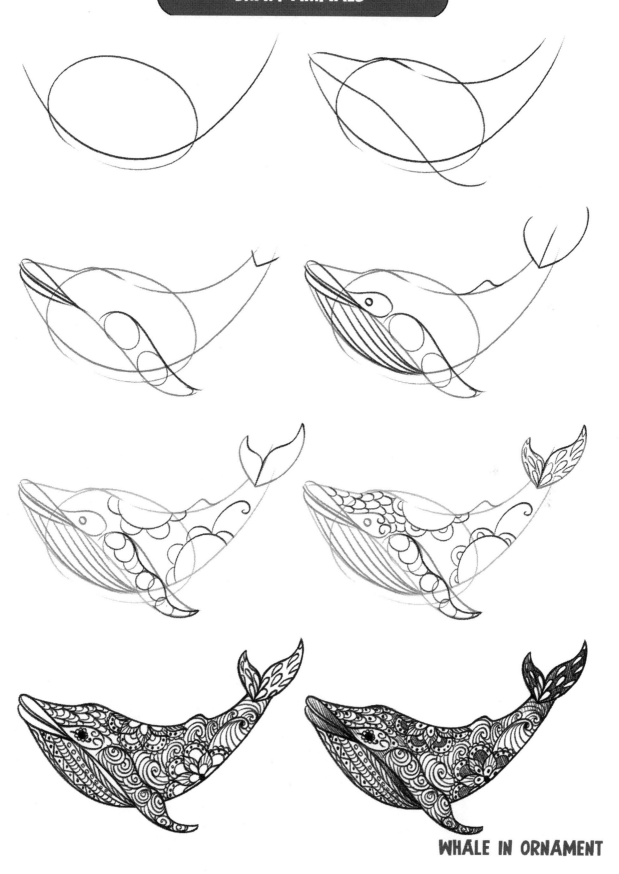

WHALE IN ORNAMENT

REALISTIC ELEPHANT ON A BALL

REALISTIC ELEPHANT ON A BALL

SNAKE

MECHANICAL RAT

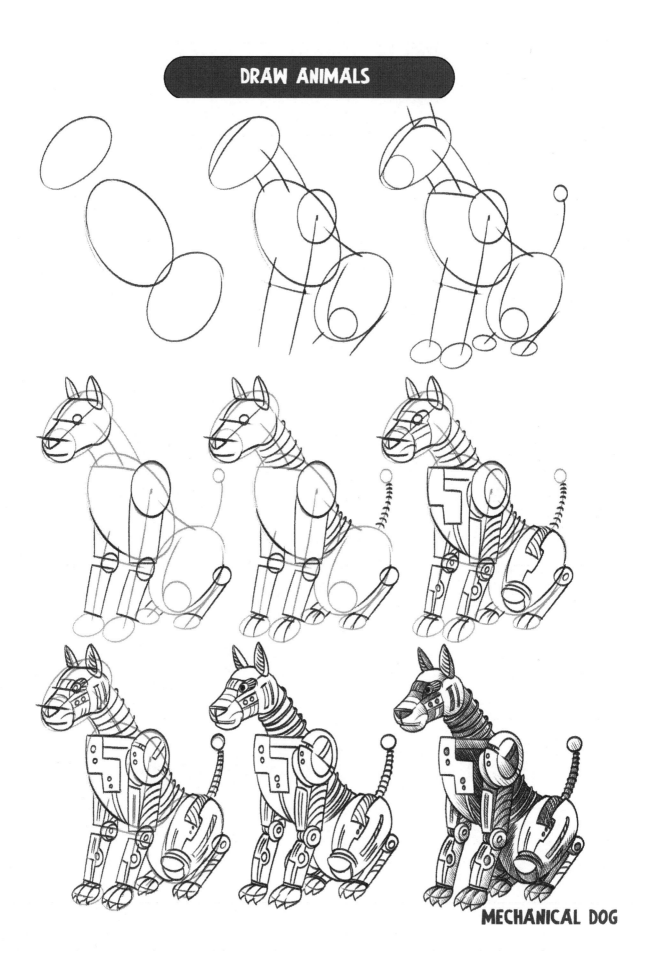

MECHANICAL DOG

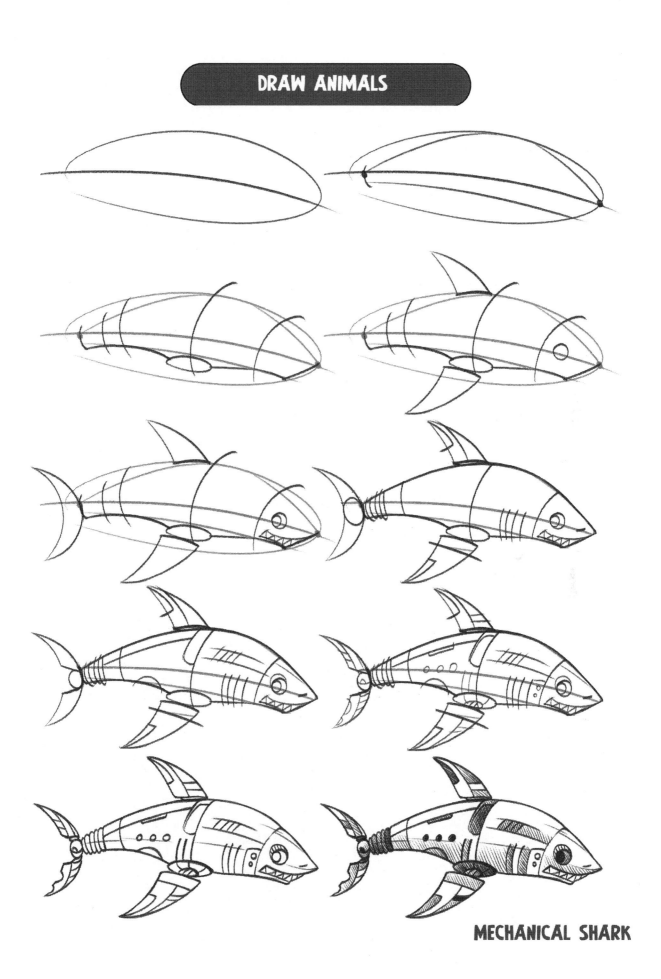

MECHANICAL SHARK

113

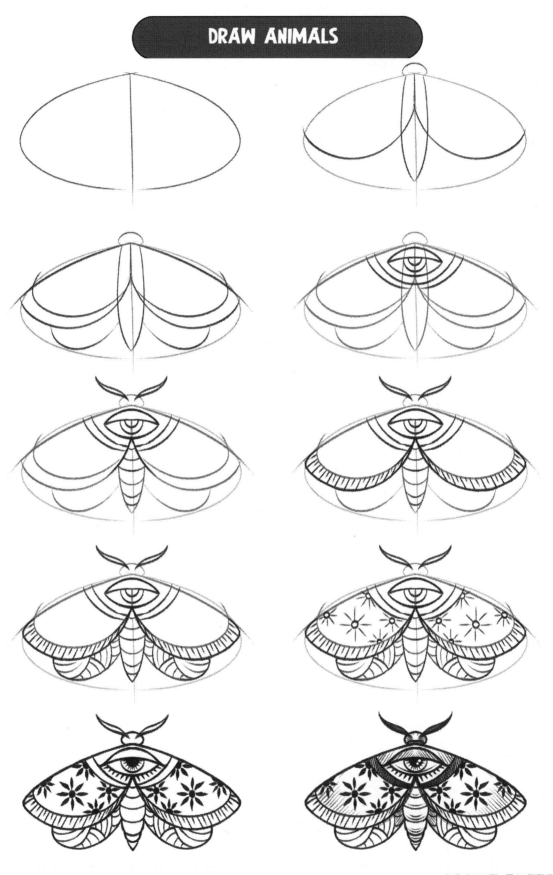

OCCULT BUTTERFLY

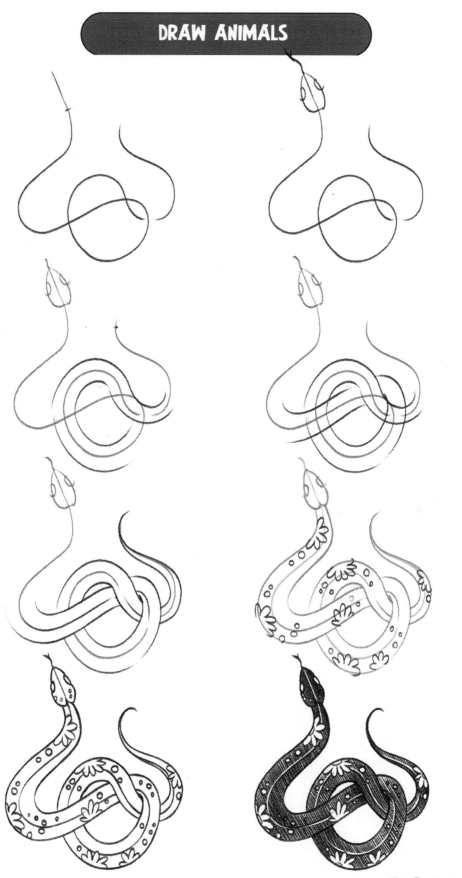

BEAUTIFUL SNAKE

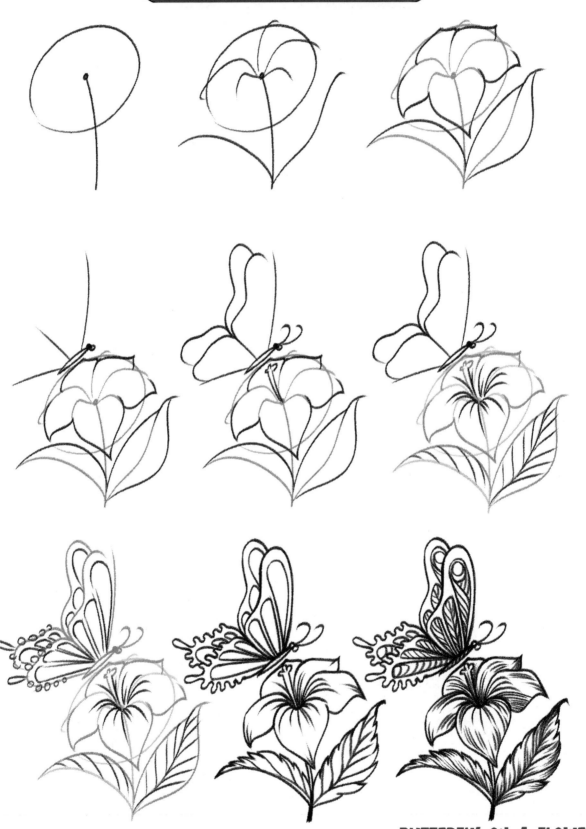

BUTTERFLY ON A FLOWER

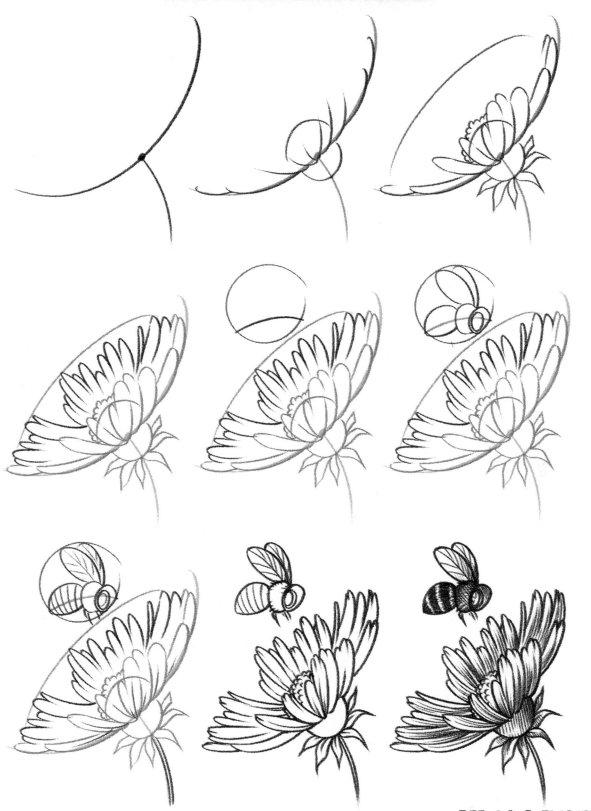

BEE ON A FLOWER

TURTLE

MUSHROOM

BEAUTIFUL DEER

BEAUTIFUL FOX

PIGEON

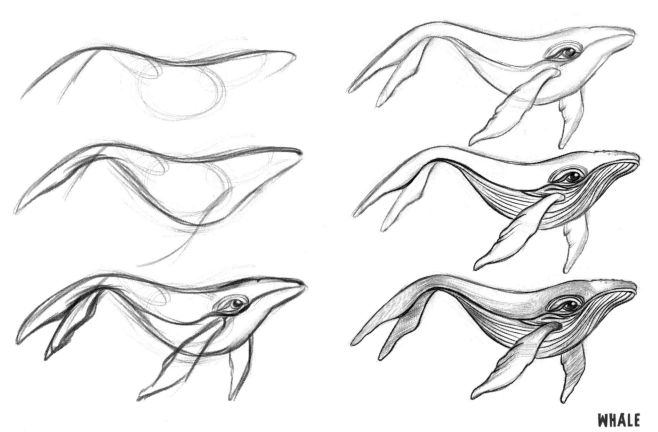

WHALE

CAT

BEAUTIFUL BUTTERFLY

MYTHICAL SKULL

BRIEFCASE

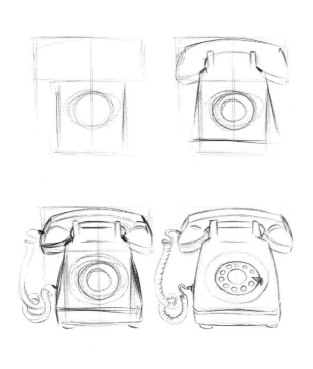

TELEPHONE

DEAR READER,

I WANT TO EXPRESS MY HEARTFELT GRATITUDE FOR CHOOSING TO BRING MY ANIME DRAWING BOOK INTO YOUR CREATIVE WORLD. YOUR SUPPORT MEANS THE WORLD TO ME. I SINCERELY HOPE THAT THE TECHNIQUES AND TIPS SHARED WITHIN THESE PAGES INSPIRE YOUR ARTISTIC JOURNEY AND BRING YOUR ANIME CREATIONS TO LIFE IN THE MOST MAGICAL WAY.

THANK YOU FOR TRUSTING IN MY GUIDANCE. HAPPY DRAWING, AND MAY YOUR IMAGINATION SOAR TO NEW HEIGHTS!

WARM REGARDS,

PATRICIA ROGERS

Made in the USA
Las Vegas, NV
21 November 2024

12327965R00070